ALA FILING RULES

Filing Committee

Resources and Technical
Services Division

American Library
Association

AMERICAN LIBRARY ASSOCIATION
Chicago
2002

Library of Congress Cataloging in Publication Data

American Library Association.   Filing Committee.
   ALA filing rules.

   Includes index.
   1. Alphabeting.   I. Title.
Z695.95.A52   1980   025.3'17   80-22186
ISBN 0-8389-3255-X

Printed in the United States of America

06   05   04   03   02   18   17   16   15   14

Contents

PREFACE   ix

INTRODUCTION   1
    Development / 1
    Objectives and Significant Features / 2
    Application (General) / 3
    Application (Local) / 4
    Aids in Using Bibliographic Files / 4
        Categorical References / 5
        Specific Filing References / 5
        Arrangement Guides / 5

GENERAL RULES   9
   1. Order of Characters / 9
      1.1 Modified Letters and Diacritics / 10
      1.2 Punctuation, Signs and Symbols / 11
      1.3 Ampersand (Optional) / 13

   2. Access Points   14
      2.1 Character-by-Character Comparison / 14
          2.1.1 Exceptions to Character-by-Character Comparison / 15
          2.1.2 Name and Title Headings as Two Elements / 15
      2.2 Function of Access Point / 15
      2.3 Subarrangement of Identical Access Points / 16
          2.3.1 Subarrangement of Added Entry
                Access Points (Optional) / 19
      2.4 Treatment of Identical Access Points and Function / 21

SPECIAL RULES   22
   3. Abbreviations / 22

4. Initial Articles / 23
   4.1 Initial Articles in Name Headings / 23
   4.2 Initial Articles in Title and Topical Subject Headings / 24

5. Initials, Initialisms, and Acronyms / 26

6. Names and Prefixes / 27

7. Nonroman Alphabets / 30

8. Numerals / 30
   8.1 General Rule / 30
   8.2 Punctuation / 30
   8.3 Decimals / 31
   8.4 Fractions / 31
   8.5 Nonarabic Notation / 31
   8.6 Superscript and Subscript Numerals / 32
   8.7 Dates in a Chronological File / 34
       8.7.1 Dates Expressed in Numerals / 34
       8.7.2 Incompletely Expressed Dates / 34

9. Relators (Designators of Function) Used in Name Headings / 36
   9.1 Relators in Name Headings (Optional) / 36

10. Terms of Honor and Address / 37

APPENDIXES
   1. Modified Letters and Special Characters / 39
   2. Articles in the Nominative Case
      in Various Foreign Languages / 40

GLOSSARY   43

INDEX   47

Figures

1	Categorical reference	6
2	Specific filing reference for a group of headings	6
3	Specific filing reference for a single heading	7
4	Specific filing reference for words with variant spellings	7
5	An arrangement card	8

Tables

| 1 | Subarrangement of Records with Identical Access Points | 17 |
| 2 | Optional Subarrangement for Name Added Entries | 21 |

CONTENTS

Examples

Order of characters	9
Modifed letters	10
Punctuation, signs and symbols	11
Ampersand (without option)	13
Ampersand (with option)	13
Character-by-character comparison	14
Function of access point	15
Subarrangement of identical access points	18
Subarrangement of identical access points (with option)	19
Treatment of identical access points and function	21
Abbreviations	22
Initial articles	25
Initials, initialisms, and acronyms	26
Names and prefixes	27
Numerals — Punctuation	30
Numerals — Decimals	31
Numerals — Fractions	31
Numerals — Nonarabic	31
Numerals — Composite example	32
Dates — Numeric	34
Dates — Phrase headings	35
Relators in name headings	36
Relators in name headings (with option)	36
Terms of honor and address	37

Preface

The ALA/RTSD Filing Committee is most grateful for the assistance received from the many librarians who commented on the drafts of the FILING RULES. Both the written responses to the rules and the suggestions received at ALA conference discussions were of great value to the Committee in producing the final version.

Special appreciation is due Daniel J. Caldano of the Columbia University Libraries for preparing the computer-based copy, which greatly facilitated the revision and final editing of the rules, and to Helen Cline of ALA Publishing Services for thoughtful and valuable guidance in preparing these rules for publication.

JOSEPH A. ROSENTHAL

Introduction

The filing rules that follow offer guidelines for the arrangement of displays of bibliographic records representing library materials.

DEVELOPMENT

The rules have been developed over the course of several years by members of the Filing Committee (previously named the Computer Filing Committee) of the Resources and Technical Services Division (RTSD) of the American Library Association. The Committee's membership has from its inception included liaison representatives from the Library and Information Technology Association (formerly the Information Science and Automation Division) of ALA, the Library of Congress, and, since 1975, from the Reference and Adult Services Division of ALA.

ALA FILING RULES is the successor to *A.L.A. Rules for Filing Catalog Cards* (1942) and *ALA Rules for Filing Catalog Cards,* second edition (1968). Since the present rules are based to a much greater extent than their predecessors on the "file-as-is" principle, and since the new rules are applicable to bibliographic displays in other than card formats, the work should be considered as new, and not as another edition.

Although the Committee has examined and benefited from features of a number of filing codes, the chief point of departure for its work has been *Filing Arrangement in the Library of Congress Catalogs /* by John C. Rather. — (Washington : Library of Congress, March 1971). The present rules diverge at many points from the principles and details of the Rather work, but its articulation and presentation have been enormously valuable as a basis for the Committee's considerations.

While these rules were being developed, the Committee maintained contact with the ALA/RTSD Catalog Code Revision Committee as it contributed to the formulation of the second edition of the *Anglo-American Cataloguing Rules (AACR2)* and with the British Library Filing Rules Committee, which has been responsible for the *British Library Filing Rules*.

The present rules are intended to be applicable to the arrangement of bibliographic records regardless of the rules by which the records have been formulated. A number of the examples provided herein illustrate records based on cataloging rules other than *AACR2*. A few examples have been devised by the Committee to illustrate particular filing rules.

OBJECTIVES AND SIGNIFICANT FEATURES

The major objectives of these rules are ease of comprehension and application and successful access to displays of bibliographic records to which the filing rules have been applied. These considerations have resulted in the following features:

1. The number of rules is relatively small, and each rule is stated as briefly as possible.
2. Exceptions to the rules and, to a large extent, optional rules have been avoided.
3. The rules have been divided into two parts: General Rules and Special Rules. The Special Rules apply to situations encountered in the arrangement and display of bibliographic records which occur with relative infrequence; for the most part they are extensions of, rather than exceptions to, the General Rules.
4. The rules reflect, with very few exceptions, the "file-as-is" principle; that is, that character strings (one or more characters set off by spaces, dashes, hyphens, diagonal slashes, or periods) to be considered for filing should be considered in exactly the form and order in which they appear. This principle emphasizes the way character strings look rather than the way they sound or their meaning. Similar elements that differ in form (e.g., numbers expressed in digits and those expressed in words) are filed in different positions. The inconvenience of having sometimes to look in two places is outweighed by the fact that no special linguistic knowledge is required to find a numeral or an abbreviation when its printed form is known.
5. The basic order of filing is word by word; it follows from application of Rule 1, Order of Characters, and Rule 1.2, Punctuation. A word is defined as a character string, as specified in item 4 above.

2

APPLICATION (GENERAL)

Application of the rules will tend to produce displays of bibliographic records that can be characterized as nonhierarchical. That is, for the most part these rules do not impose structure on bibliographic displays other than that which is already implicit in, and which results from, the exercise and application of cataloging rules such as the *Anglo-American Cataloguing Rules.* This characteristic derives from the entire orientation of the filing rules, although the features that exemplify it most substantially are:

1. The stipulation that punctuation is not considered for filing purposes (Rule 1.2)
2. The omission of any distinction for filing purposes among persons, places, things, and titles when the same character string applies to different types of headings. (However, identical headings that have different functions — e.g., main entries and subject entries — are distinguished for filing purposes; cf. Rule 2.2.)

Some effects may be anticipated as a result of these features. Searching in a file for specific items for which one or more access points (e.g., author, title, series) are precisely known should be generally facilitated because there will be no need to consider punctuation or to distinguish the categories of persons, places, things, and titles. On the other hand, access points related by such factors as entry under place (e.g., *London. Institute of Child Health.* and *London. Metropolitan Board of Works.*) may be separated in a display by quite unrelated headings (*London, Jack, 1876–1916.*). Similarly, in a file that includes various types of access points, subdivisions under a single subject heading (e.g., *Silver — Assaying* and *Silver — Metallurgy*) may be separated by access points with different functions (*Silver, Harold* or *The silver chalice*).

Librarians and others responsible for the arrangement of records in bibliographic displays may well wish to institute or retain principles of filing that group access points related by characteristics such as those illustrated above. Most sets of filing rules issued and widely available up to this time produce this result. Some examples of such sets of rules follow:

ALA Rules for Filing Catalog Cards / prepared by the ALA Editorial Committee's Subcommittee on the ALA Rules for Filing Catalog Cards; Pauline A. Seeley, chairman and editor. — 2nd ed. — Chicago : American Library Association, 1968.

Library of Congress Filing Rules / prepared by John C. Rather and Susan C. Biebel — Washington : Library of Congress, 1980.

The present rules are intended to be applicable to the arrangement of bibliographic records, whether by manual or automated means. Although the Committee was initially constituted as the Computer Filing Committee of RTSD, and although it has frequently had occasion to consider machine-related developments (MARC formats for bibliographic records, varying forms of bibliographic data display made possible through photocomposition, computer-output microform, and cathode-ray tube terminals), its major considerations have rested in the area of human utilization of bibliographic files.

APPLICATION (LOCAL)

As previously implied, each possible application of these rules should be considered in the context of a particular institution's files and bibliographic needs. Rearrangement of an existing file in manual form (i.e., a card catalog) that has been ordered on the basis of hierarchically oriented filing rules would in all probability involve a considerable expenditure of time and effort. Developments in North American libraries in the 1970s have, however, brought the beginnings of a large number of new bibliographic displays in various forms (book, microform, and on-line as well as card catalogs), with the likelihood of many more occurring in 1981 or soon thereafter. The present rules may be of particular interest and value for the arrangement of records in such files.

AIDS IN USING BIBLIOGRAPHIC FILES

The major principles and features of the present rules should be comprehensible to regular users of files in which the rules are applied. For even regular users, however, guidance and assistance may be necessary, and for new or occasional users, it may be particularly important to provide a system of explanatory and illustrative devices. The following types of aids may be useful.

1. A brief version of the essential rules. It should probably be limited to one or two pages, and thus be made conveniently available as a handout, as well as posted prominently in the area of the files. In the case of book or microform catalogs, the brief form might be included as an initial page or frame in the bibliographic product and might be made easily available for reference in using an on-line display.

2. Information notices and references. Three types that may be

4

valuable are: categorical references, specific filing references, and arrangement guides. These may be interspersed at appropriate points in the bibliographic file.

Categorical References. A categorical reference briefly explains a particular rule, describes its effect on entries in variant forms, and points to other parts of the file where these entries may be found. By functioning as a general reference for a category of headings (e.g., those beginning with a numeral), a categorical reference lessens the need for specific filing references. Figure 1 gives an example of a categorical reference. This type of aid is filed with sizable groups of entries under variant forms of the same item. For example, the explanation of the treatment of numbers belongs with entries beginning with numerals and with groups of entries beginning with specific numbers expressed in words (e.g., *one, one hundred*).

In any form of bibliographic display (card catalog, book catalog, microform catalog, on-line display) care should be taken to provide categorical references at appropriate points in the display and to format them in such a way as to call attention to their function as guides. For example, arrangement cards and categorical references in a card catalog may be printed on 3¼-by-5-inch stock with the caption along the top edge so that they protrude above neighboring cards. One categorical reference of any given kind is usually sufficient for a catalog drawer.

Categorical references may be made to explain filing practices applied to the following features of any extensive display of bibliographic records: abbreviations; hyphenated words (filed under common prefixes); initials and acronyms (only at points in the display where entries are filed as separate letters); names with prefixes (filed under common prefixes); and numerals. The need for other categorical references depends on the structure and size of a given file.

Specific Filing References. A reference may be made for a specific heading or group of headings, the location of which might be unexpected or difficult to find for users accustomed to other filing rules and arrangements. Such a reference is made by reconstructing the heading so that the reference can be filed by the rules in a desired alternative location. Figure 2 gives an example of a filing reference for a group of headings; figure 3 exemplifies a filing reference for a single heading; figure 4 exemplifies a filing reference for words with variant spellings. This type of aid supplements references from alternative forms of heading required by cataloging rules.

Arrangement Guides. The arrangement of entries under certain headings (typically uniform titles and voluminous authors) is frequently so complex that a user may be expected to require assistance in accessing

Information Card: Treatment of Numbers

   Numbers expressed as numerals (e.g., 4, 1984, XX)
precede words consisting of letters, and are arranged
according to their numerical value (roman numerals
are treated like arabic numerals).
   Numbers expressed as words (e.g., four, nineteen
eighty-four, twenty) are filed alphabetically.
   If you do not find what you want in this portion
of the catalog, look under the alternative form.
When looking for a number expressed as a word, bear
in mind that the number may be written in any of
several ways (e.g., one hundred, a hundred) which
file in different places in the catalog.

Figure 1. Categorical reference

U.S.   Army.   Infantry

   Entries for headings with a numeral before the
last part of this heading (e.g., U.S.   Army.   1st
Infantry) are in the group of headings arranged in
numerical order after subject headings for U.S.   Army
and before headings beginning U.S.   Army.   A...

Figure 2. Specific filing reference for a group of headings

```
Colour

    Entry words spelled in different ways, e.g.,
"Color" and "Colour", are filed under the form as
spelled.  If you do not find what you want in this
portion of the catalog, look under the alternative
spelling.
```

Figure 3. Specific filing reference for a single heading

```
TREES--WEST

    see

    TREES--THE WEST    [Articles at the beginning
                        of subdivisions are
                        regarded in filing]
```

Figure 4. Specific filing reference for words with variant spellings

particular records included under such headings. Subarrangements may result naturally from the structuring of uniform titles that include terms denoting language, portion(s) of a work (e.g., *Bible. Old Testament*), or publication data. To assist users, the provision of an outline of the subarrangement at the beginning of listings under such headings is recommended. In a long file (such as entries for the Bible), it may be desirable to intersperse several such notices or guides at strategic points. Figure 5 gives an example of an arrangement guide in card form.

```
Goethe, Johann Wolfgang von, 1749-1832

     Entries under this heading are grouped as follows:
     Works written, edited, or translated by the author
and works to which he contributed in some other
manner are arranged by title.  Collective uniform
titles (Correspondence, Plays, Works, etc.) are filed
alphabetically among individual titles.
     Under each title, the groupings are as follows:
1) editions in the original language and added
entries for related works, by date; 2) works about
the title, by author, title, and date; 3) translations
of the work, by language and date.
     Works about the author are arranged by author of
the work, title, and date.
```

Figure 5. An arrangement card

General Rules

1.   ORDER OF CHARACTERS

The basic order of characters to be considered in comparing data elements in bibliographic records for filing purposes is as follows:

> Spaces, dashes, hyphens, diagonal slashes, periods
>> All characters in this group have equal filing value. Multiple consecutive spaces and their equivalents are to be compressed to a single space. However, all spaces and their equivalents that precede the first alphabetic or numeric character in a data element are ignored.[1] Apply the principle "nothing files before something," with spaces and their equivalents being considered as nothing.
>
> Numerals: 0 through 9
>> All character strings beginning with numerals are arranged before character strings beginning with letters.
>
> Letters of the English alphabet: A through Z
>> Lowercase and uppercase letters have equal filing value.
>
> Letters of nonroman alphabets (*see* Rule 7)

EXAMPLES:
> (Subject headings used as examples in these rules appear in all upper-case letters.)

> 26 ways of looking at a black man
> 44 Irish short stories
> A-5 rocket

---

1. For purposes of these rules, the word *ignored* signifies that the space, mark, or character to be ignored is treated as if it did not exist. It is not to be treated as if it were a space.

A.J.S. motorcycle
A priori arguments
Aarhus, Denmark

HAND—ANATOMY
HAND IN ART
HAND-TO-HAND FIGHTING
HAND WASHING
HAND—WOUND AND INJURIES
HANDBAGS

O, Chae-ho
O.R.U.N.
OAU/STRC
OAU today
One hundred years of brewing
OPT, the magazine on people and things

Ten modern New Zealand poets
Theory of plasmas
Thirty years that shook physics

1.1　Modified Letters and Diacritics
Modified letters are treated like their plain equivalents in the English alphabet. All diacritical marks associated with, and modifications to, recognizable English letters are ignored. (Appendix 1 lists modified letters and special characters.)

EXAMPLES:
Aasland, Tertit
Aasma, Felix
Aastrom, Jeppe
Aav, Yrjo
Åslander, Alfred
Ástrom, Lara
Aström, Margit

Muehlberger, Clarence Weinert
Muehlner, Mrs. Susanne
Muel, Leon
Mueller, Alfred Don
Mühler, Heinrich von
Mülen, Laurenz von der
Mulholland, John
Müllen, Lyder von
Mullen, Pat

10

Muller, Arnold
Müller, Carl Otto

Nevves from America
Nevves of Sʳ Walter Rauleigh
Newes from New-England
Newest England

Oeri, Albert
Oerlein, Karl Ferdinand
Oertel, Felix
Örne, Anders
Ørsted, Hans Christian
Örström, Olof Valfrid
Osler, Sir William

Slonimskaĭa, Mariĭa
Słonimski, Antoni
Slonimskiĭ, Ivan
Slow learners
Słowakische Nationalgalerie
Słownik geodezyjny
Slowo o Leninie
Slowpoke

1.2   Punctuation, Signs and Symbols

Punctuation and all nonalphabetic signs and symbols (except as noted in Rules 1, 1.3, and 8.2) are ignored for filing purposes.

EXAMPLES:
$$$ and sense
B . . . . . ch, A.
B*** de B***
B . . . . des E . . . , J. F. A.
B — —s
B — —t — —n, Richard
B — —vie, B.
Ba, Amadou
Boys' clubs
Boys of '76
Boy's town
Budget planning
C., A. J.
C# ballard
Campbell and Mitchell, firm, booksellers
Campbell, Arthur
Campbell-Bannerman, Sir Henry

Campbell, Charles
Campbell-Copeland, Thomas
CAMPBELL COUNTY, TENNESSEE
Campbell family
Campbell University, Holton, Kansas
Campbell, William Giles
Campbell, William Wallace
Christmas Carol
***, countess of
Design of a precision integrator
Dollars and sense
E.J.W. Bibb memorial series
E.M.F. electrical yearbook
E pluribus unum
E.S. Montague; a study
ELH: a journal of English . . .
¥ $ £ exchange tables
Exchange torque, power and momentum flow
John and Mary
John/Paul/George/Ringo
John Paul Jones
Le Strange, Guy
L'Estrange, Alfred
L'Estrange, Roger
LIFE
Life; a book for young men
Life — a bowl of rice
Life after death
Life — an obstacle race
Life and art
LIFE (BIOLOGY)
LIFE-BOATS
Life, mind and spirit
LIFE — ORIGIN
Life; outline of general biology
LIFE, VALUE OF
Lloyd family
Lloyd George and the war
Lloyd-James, Arthur
Lloyd, Matheson and Carritt
Lloyd-Williams, Richard
Manual on aeroelasticity
†mas star for the poor
Massachusetts Institute of Technology
— — —ö— — —ö— — —, see . . .
% of gain

12

─ ─ on, Nicolas
Study of the ammonia molecule in the interstellar medium
Study of the Υ - Deexcitation
Study of the dipion system . . .
Trans-atlantic
Transafrican
Transportation
Vision plus value series
Vision research
Vision + value series
Who is who in music
Who'd be king
Whom the gods destroy
Who's who in America
Whose sea
Xmas star for the poor

1.3 Ampersand (Optional)

The ampersand (&) is filed as its spelled-out language equivalent.

EXAMPLES
(without option):
A Alfonso Reyes, 17 de
  Mayo de 1949
A and G motor vehicle
A and P Company
A & B Internationale
A & B poetry
A &c
A estrêla sobe
A. F., ed.
A & O International
A & O Österreich
A un joven socialista
  mexicano
A und O
A une courtisane
$$$ and sense
Art and beauty
Art & commonsense
Arte and crafte
Arte & beautye
Arte & cultura   [Italian]
Arte & cultura   [Spanish]
Arte e arqueologia
Arte e historia

EXAMPLES
(with option)
A Alfonso Reyes, 17 de
  Mayo de 1949
A & B poetry
A and G motor vehicle
A & O International
A and P Company
A estrêla sobe
A & B Internationale [& filed as *et*]
A. F., ed.
A un joven socialista
  mexicano
A und O
A & O Österreich [& filed as *und*]
A une courtisane
$$$ and sense
Art and beauty
Art & commonsense
Art &c. [&c filed as *etc.*]
Arte & beautye [& filed as *and*]
Arte and crafte
Arte e arqueologia
Arte & cultura [& filed as *e*]
Arte e historia
Arte & cultura [& filed as *y*]

13

2. ACCESS POINTS

In any display of bibliographic records, the records appear under one or more access points, often referred to as headings or entries. Major categories of access points include author, title, added entries, series, and subject entries, i.e., the data elements included in MARC fields 1XX, 2XX (except 250, 260–65), 4XX (except 490), 6XX, 7XX and 8XX.[2]

The access point under which the record is to be displayed should receive primary consideration.

2.1 Character-by-Character Comparison

In order to arrange records with access points that are not identical, the access points are compared character by character according to the order of characters specified in Rule 1.

> EXAMPLES:
> London and Londoners
> London, Andrea
> London as it is today
> LONDON BRIDGE
> London bridge is falling down
> London Conference on . . .
> LONDON (CRUISER)
> London, Declaration of, 1909
> LONDON (DOG)
> LONDON (ENGLAND) – ANTIQUITIES
> London (England).   Conference on . . .
> London (England).   County Council.
> LONDON (ENGLAND) – DESCRIPTION
> LONDON (ENGLAND : DIOCESE)
> London (England).   Guild Hall
> London (England).   International Conference on . . .
> LONDON (ENGLAND) – POLITICS AND GOVERNMENT
> London (England).   Royal School of Mines
> London (England).   Symposium on . . .
> London (England).   University
> London, Jack
> London (Ky.)
> London, O. W. H.
> London Old Boy's Association
> London (Ont.)
> LONDON (ONT.) – HISTORY
> London Shakespeare League
> London, Thomas
> LONDON TOWER
> LONDON, TREATY OF, 1915
> London, yesterday, today, and tomorrow

2. United States. Library of Congress. Automated Systems Office. *MARC formats for bibliographic data.* — Washington, D.C. : Library of Congress, 1980.

2.1.1   Exceptions to Character-by-Character Comparison

In this and any character-by-character comparison for the purpose of arranging bibliographic records, each character is to be regarded in exactly the form and order in which it appears. Principal exceptions to this rule are cited in Rule 4.2 (Initial Articles), Rules 8.2–8.7.2 (Numerals), Rule 9 (Relators Used in Name Headings), and Rule 10 (Terms of Honor and Address).

2.1.2   Name and Title Headings as Two Elements

Access points consisting of the heading for a personal or corporate name and a title, such as

Aristoteles.   Metaphysica.
Society for Pure English.   Tract no. 36.
Homer.   Iliad.

are treated as though they consist of two separate data elements. Thus the title portion files with all other titles under the same name heading.

2.2   Function of Access Point

In order to arrange bibliographic records having identical access points, the function of the access point (or, in the case of references, the function of the entire record) is considered first. On this basis, records are ordered by the following categories:

Explanatory, "see" and "see also" references for main and added (including series) entries
Main and added (including series) entries interfiled
Explanatory, "see" and "see also" references for subject entries
Subject entries.

EXAMPLES:
Philadelphia as it is
Philadelphia.   Athenaeum
PHILADELPHIA.   ATHENAEUM
Philadelphia.   Centennial Exhibition, 1876
PHILADELPHIA.   CENTENNIAL EXHIBITION, 1876
PHILADELPHIA.   CENTENNIAL EXHIBITION, 1876 –
   BRAZIL
Philadelphia.   Centennial memorial of American independence
PHILADELPHIA CO., PA. – BIOGRAPHY
Philadelphia Co., Pa.   Committee of the Third Battalion District
Philadelphia.   Councils. *see also*
Philadelphia.   Councils
Philadelphia.   Free Library
PHILADELPHIA.   FREE LIBRARY
Philadelphia.   Free Library.   Rare Book Dept.
PHILADELPHIA.   FREE LIBRARY.   THOMAS HOLME
   BRANCH

Philadelphia.   Independence Hall
PHILADELPHIA.   INDEPENDENCE HALL
Philadelphia.   Independence Hall.   National Museum
PHILADELPHIA METROPOLITAN AREA
Philadelphia metropolitan economy
PHILADELPHIA — PUBLIC BUILDINGS
Philadelphia.   Public Buildings Commission
PHILADELPHIA — RIOTS, 1844
The Philadelphia riots of 1844

2.3   Subarrangement of Identical Access Points

The arrangement of records having identical access points, and equivalent functions, is determined by consideration of secondary data elements. The order of data elements to be considered is:

Group A (records with author or uniform title main entry)

1) Author or uniform title main entry
2) Title[3]
3) Date of publication, distribution, etc.

Group B (records with title main entry other than uniform title main entry)

1) Title main entry[4]
2) Date of publication, distribution, etc.

If the access point is a personal or corporate name added entry, in Group A the access point replaces the main entry. In Group B, the name added entry is considered before the title main entry for filing consideration.

If the access point is a title added entry, in Group A the access point is considered before the main entry, and the title is not considered. In Group B, the title added entry replaces the title main entry.

If the access point is a subject or a series added entry, the access point is considered before the main entry in Group A or Group B for filing consideration. Note: A name-title subject or series added entry is treated as two data elements (Rule 2.1.2); both are regarded before the main entry in Group A or Group B.

---

3. If more than one title element is present, choose one of the following in the order prescribed:

Uniform or filing title (MARC field 240, 243)
Romanized title (MARC field 241)
Title proper (MARC field 245)

4. Same as footnote 3.

2.3 SUBARRANGEMENT OF IDENTICAL ACCESS POINTS

If the access point is a name-title added entry that is not a subject entry or a series entry, the access point replaces the main entry and title elements in Group A, or the main entry in Group B, for filing consideration.

Additionally, if an added entry access point contains a date of publication, distribution, etc., that date replaces the date of publication, distribution, etc., in Group A or Group B for filing consideration.

Table 1 illustrates Rule 2.3 for the most commonly encountered access points. The MARC tags given in this table are illustrative and not exhaustive.

TABLE 1. SUBARRANGEMENT OF RECORDS WITH IDENTICAL ACCESS POINTS

Access Point	Subarrangement		
	1st	2nd	3rd
Name main entry. MARC 1XX (except 130)	Title. $t if present, or 240, 243, 241, 245	Date of pub., dist., etc. 260 $c	
Uniform title main entry. MARC 130	Title. 243, 241, 245	Date of pub., dist., etc. 260 $c	
Title main entry. MARC 245	Date of pub., dist., etc. 260 $c		
Name added entry. MARC 700, 711	Title. $t if present, or 240, 243, 241, 245	Date of pub., dist., etc. 260 $c	
Title added entry. MARC 245, 730, 740	Author or uniform title main entry, if any. MARC 1XX	Date of pub., dist., etc. 260 $c	
Series added entry.[1] MARC 4XX (except 490), 800–840	Author or uniform title main entry, if any. MARC 1XX	Title. 240, 243, 241, 245	Date of pub., dist., etc. 260 $c
Subject added entry.[2] MARC 6XX	Author or uniform title main entry, if any. MARC 1XX	Title. 240, 243, 241, 245	Date of pub., dist., etc. 260 $c

1. If a series added entry or a subject added entry consists of an author *and* a title, treat them as two separate data elements (cf. Rule 2.1.2).
2. Same as note 1.

When selecting the data elements for subarrangement, only one element should be chosen from each column. For example, if the access point is a name added entry heading, the first element of subarrangement is the title subfield if it is present in the added entry. If it is not present, select one of the following fields in the order listed: 240, 243, 241, 245.

EXAMPLES:
Hamilton, Alexander, 1712–1756.
  Gentleman's progress.

Hamilton, Alexander, 1739–1802
  A treatise on the management of . . .

Hamilton, Alexander, 1757–1804
Hall, Margaret Esther, 1905– ed.
  Alexander Hamilton reader; a compilation . . .

Hamilton, Alexander, 1757–1804
  Colonel Hamilton's second letter . . .

Hamilton, Alexander, 1757–1804. Defense of Mr. Jay's Treaty.
The American remembrancer; or, An impartial . . .

Hamilton, Alexander, 1757–1804
  The fate of Major Andre; . . .

HAMILTON, ALEXANDER, 1757–1804. A FULL VINDICA-
  TION OF THE MEASURES OF CONGRESS.
Seabury, Samuel, Bp., 1729–1796
  Letters of a Westchester farmer . . .

HAMILTON, ALEXANDER, 1757–1804. A FULL VINDICA-
  TION OF THE MEASURES OF CONGRESS.
Seabury, Samuel, Bp., 1729–1796
  A view of the controversy between . . .

Hamilton, Alexander, 1757–1804
  Genl. Alexander Hamilton's confidential letter . . .

Hamilton, Alexander, 1757–1804
Jefferson, Thomas, pres., U.S., 1743–1826
  Jeffersonian principles and Hamiltonian principles.

Hamilton, Alexander, 1757–1804
  Letters of Pacificus : written in justification . . . 1796.

Hamilton, Alexander, 1757–1804. Letters of Pacificus
The Federalist.
  The Federalist on the new Constitution . . . 1831.

Hamilton, Alexander, 1757–1804
[Selections.]
Alexander Hamilton and Thomas Jefferson . . . 1943.

Hamilton, Alexander, 1757–1804
[Selections.]
The basic ideas of Alexander Hamilton . . . 1957.

Hamilton, Alexander, 1757–1804
[Works.]
The works of Alexander Hamilton . . . 1810.

Hamilton, Alexander, 1757–1804. Works.
American Review of history and politics.
The works of Alexander Hamilton . . . 1811.

Hamilton, Alexander, 1757–1804
[Works.]
The papers of Alexander Hamilton . . . 1915–1917.

HAMILTON, ALEXANDER, 1757–1804
Flexner, James Thomas, 1908–
The Young Hamilton

Hamilton, Alexander, pseud. *see* Shiman, Russell Gardner

2.3.1 Subarrangement of Added Entry Access Points (Optional)

The following alternative arrangement may be followed for records displayed under added entry access points, when a nondistinctive or collective uniform title is present (MARC fields 240 or 243), as in the case of added entries for performers of musical compositions. If the access point is a name added entry, the name added entry is considered first, followed by the main entry, then the uniform title. (See table 2, page 21.)

EXAMPLES:
Badura-Skoda, Paul, 1927–
Haydn, Joseph, 1732–1809
[Sonata, piano, no. 52, E major] Phonodisc.
Sonate Es-dur. Sonate h-mol. Variationen f-moll. Harmonia Mundi HM 30 634. [196–]

Badura-Skoda, Paul, 1927–
Martin, Frank, 1890–1974
[Concerto, violin] Phonodisc.
Concerto for violin and orchestra. Second piano concerto. Candide CE31055. [1972]

Badura-Skoda, Paul, 1927–

Mozart, Johann Chrysostom Wolfgang Amadeus, 1756–1791
[Works, piano, 4 hands] Phonodisc.
The complete 4-hand piano music.   Musical Heritage Society MHS
1293–1296.   [1972]

Badura-Skoda, Paul, 1927–
Schubert, Franz Peter, 1797–1828
[Quintet, piano, violin, viola, violoncello & double-bass, D.667,
A major] Phonodisc.
Trout quintet, A major, op. 114.   Westminster WL 50–25. [cover
c1950]

Badura-Skoda, Paul, 1927–
Schubert, Franz Peter, 1797–1828
[Quintet, piano, violin, viola, violoncello & double-bass, D.667,
A major] Phonodisc.
Quintet in A major, op.114 (The "Trout") Westminster XWN 18264.
[c1956]

Badura-Skoda, Paul, 1927–
Schubert, Franz Peter, 1797–1828
[Trio, piano & strings, D.898, B♭ major] Phonodisc.
Trio no. 1 in B flat major, op.99, for piano and strings.   West-
minster XWN 18481.   [1957]

Badura-Skoda, Paul, 1927–
Schubert, Franz Peter, 1797–1828
[Trio, piano & strings, D.929, E♭ major] Phonodisc.
Trio in E flat major, op.100.   Westminster WL 5121.   [c1952]

Badura-Skoda, Paul, 1927–
Schubert, Franz Peter, 1797–1828
[Trio, piano & strings, D.929, E♭ major] Phonodisc.
Trio in E flat major, op.100, for piano and strings.   Westminster
XWN 18482.   [1957]

Badura-Skoda, Paul, 1927–
Schubert, Franz Peter, 1797–1828
[Variationen über ein Original-Thema, piano 4 hands, D.813, A♭
major] Phonodisc.
Variations in A flat major, op.35, for piano four hands.   Variations in B flat major, op.82, no.2, for piano four hands. Lebens-
stürme, op.144, for piano four hands. Westminster WL 5147. [c1952]

Badura-Skoda, Paul, 1927–
Schumann, Robert Alexander, 1810–1856.
[Sonata, piano, no.1, op.11, F# minor] Phonodisc.
Sonata, no. 1, in F sharp minor, op.11. Carnaval, op.9.
Westminster WL 5105. [c1951]

TABLE 2. OPTIONAL SUBARRANGEMENT FOR NAME ADDED ENTRIES

Access Point	Subarrangement		
	1st	2nd	3rd
Name added entry. MARC 700, 711	Main entry. 1XX	Uniform title. 240 or 243	Date of pub., dist., etc. 260 $c

2.4 Treatment of Identical Access Points and Function

If all the data elements considered for filing in two or more records are identical and the records have equivalent functions, then the records file at random.

EXAMPLES:
Light (Motion picture) 1957
Light (Motion picture) 1965
Light (Motion picture) 1968
Light (Motion picture) 1969
Light (Motion picture) 1969
Light (Motion picture) 1969

Special Rules

3. **ABBREVIATIONS**

Abbreviations are arranged exactly as written.

EXAMPLES:

C.I.B.   [reference]
C.I.B. bulletin
C/O Colby
CdS crystals
Ce que je crois
CeBeDem   *see* . . .
CO_2: chemical, biochemical, and physiological aspects
CO_2 lasers
Coal as an energy resource
Col. Clayton's lake tour
Cole, Bruce
Collection de logique mathématique
Colonel Thorndyke's secret

Doctor Bard of Hyde Park
Doktor Brents Wandlung
Doktor, Raphael
Dr. Austin's guests

. . . et ce fut la guerre
Et cetera; a collector's scrap-book
Et in Arcadia ego
Etc.
Etch proofs

K. Akademie der Wissenschaften, Berlin
K. K. Akademie der bildenden Künste, Vienna

22

K. K. Hof- und Staatsdruckerei, Austria
König, Georg
Königlicher Botanischer Garten, Munich
Koninklijk Institut voor de Tropen

M. Gallet
Madame Maillart
Mademoiselle's hats
Messieurs Sansan
Mis' Stone and other Vermont monologues
Misadventures of a tropical medico
Mister Fish Kelly
Mistress Anne
Mladenov, Stefen
Mlle. Henriette
MM. Poule, Laigre & c^{ie}
Mme. Maimée
Monsieur Beaucaire
Mr. Deeds Goes to Town
Mrs. Miniver
Ms.   [periodical]
MSS. (Rothschild 2973)

No.   [title of a book]
No and yes
No, Fernando Lorenti de
NO (JAPANESE DRAMA AND THEATER)
Number 8 John Street
Number concept

R. Accademia filarmonica, Bologna
Real Seminario de Nobles de Vergara
Regia Galleria di Firenze illustrata
Royal, George

Saint-Lambert, Michel de
Sainte-Foi, Charles
St. Louis, Henri
St. Louis (Mo., U.S.)
Staack, John George
Ste. Genevieve (Mo., U.S.)
Steacy, Frederick William

4.   INITIAL ARTICLES
4.1   Initial Articles in Name Headings
Initial articles that form an integral part of place name and personal name headings (including nicknames, sobriquets, and phrases char-

acterizing persons) are regarded for filing purposes at the beginning of the following access points:

Access Point	MARC Field
Personal name	100, 400, 600, 700, 800
Corporate name	110, 410, 610, 710, 810
Conference or meeting	111, 411, 611, 711, 811
Geographic name	651, 652, 752

Disregard initial articles at the beginning of corporate name headings other than those beginning with personal and place names.

4.2   Initial Articles in Title and Topical Subject Headings

Initial articles in the nominative case are ignored at the beginning of the following access points, whether they appear separately or are elided.[5] For articles occurring in place names and personal names that begin a title, follow Rule 4.1.

Access Point	MARC Field	MARC Subfield
Uniform title	130, 240, 243, 630, 730, 830	$a
Romanized title	241	$a
Translation of title by cataloging agency	242	$a
Title	210, 212, 245, 246, 247	$a
Topical subject	650	$a
Title traced differently	740	$a
Series added entry title	440, 840	$a
Title in name/title entry	XXX	$t

Appendix 2 lists definite and indefinite articles in frequently encountered languages in the nominative case only (all genders both singular and plural), which should be disregarded whenever they occur as the initial word of a title or topical subject heading. In languages having an indefinite article, the word or words representing the cardinal numeral one also are given whenever the same form is used. An initial numeral, whether used as a noun or an adjective, must always be regarded in filing. (Note that there are no articles, either definite or indefinite, in Czech, Estonian, Finnish, Latin, Latvian, Lithuanian, Polish, Russian, Serbo-Croatian, Slovak, Slovenian, and Ukrainian.)

5. Articles at the beginning of subdivisions of access points are regarded in filing.

4.2 INITIAL ARTICLES IN TITLE AND TOPICAL SUBJECT HEADINGS

EXAMPLES:

American, pseud.
  A journal of a tour of Italy
An American   [initial article regarded
  The amazing America   in personal name]
An American
  Constantinople and its environs
Anderson, John

Cluain Éanna urís
The Club.   [title. Imprint date: 1932]
Der Club.   [title. Imprint date: 1955]
A Club.
  Annals of A Club, 1764–1914
Club 21, New York   [reference]
Club accounts
The Club, London
The Club, New Haven
The Club, Rochester

El-Abiad, Ahmed H., 1926–
El Al Israel airlines
El Alamein
el-Ayooty, Eisha Yassin Mohamed
El-Baz, Edgard, 1937–
El-Baz, Farouk
El Campo, Tex.
El Curioso parlante   [reference]
The El Dorado Trail   [title]
El, ella y el otro
El Greco
El in the Ugaritic texts

La Fontaine, Jean de, 1621–1695
Las de los sombreros verdos
Las Hurdes, Spain
Laš, Michal
Las que llegaron después
Las Vegas Valley
Las Vergnas, Georges
Lasa, José Maria de

TREES—THE WEST
TREES—UNITED STATES

THE WEST
West African bounty
THE WEST—ANTIQUITIES
West, William

25

5. INITIALS, INITIALISMS, AND ACRONYMS

Consideration of initials, initialisms, and acronyms for filing purposes is governed by Rule 1, which specifies order of characters. Initials, initialisms, and acronyms separated by spaces, dashes, hyphens, diagonal slashes, or periods are regarded as separate words. Initials, initialisms, and acronyms in which characters are separated only by other marks or symbols, or which are not separated in any way, are regarded as single words.

EXAMPLES:

I-90 design team
I-95 harbor crossing corridor study
I., A.
I.A.A.
I.A.G. Literature on automation
I.A.M. Symposia on Microbiology
I am a mathematician
I and CS: the magazine of instruments . . .
I.B.   ["see" reference]
I., B.
   Brief discovrs dedié av Roy . . .
I.B.R.O.   ["see also" reference]
I built a bridge, and other poems
I.C.A. Congress
I.C.E. abstracts
I.C.I.
I Ch'ien
I chose freedom
I.D.A.
I.E.
I.E.E.E.   ["see also" reference]
I.E.E.E. Acoustics, Speech, and Signal Processing Society
I.E.E.E.-G.M.M.S. E.R.S. Symposium
I.F.I.P. Colloquium on Optimization Techniques
I & LR monograph series
I & M Section on Automatic Control, Stockholm
I.N.T.E.L.S.A.T.
I.O.N. Astrodynamics Specialist Conference
The I.Q. Controversy
I.R.E. Instrumentation Conference
I.R.E. P.G.C.S.
IAMPA Symposia on Long-term Climatic Fluctuations
I***B
IBI-ICC International Symposium

26

IBM   ["see also" reference]
IBM 1130/1800 basic FORTRAN IV language
IBM 1130 disc monitor system
IBM application program
IBRO bulletin
IC master
ICFTU/IFBWW International Housing Committee
ICFTU monographs
IECI-IAS Technical Conference
IEE journal on electronic circuits and systems
IEEE/AIAA Thermoelectric Specialists Conference
IEEE G-ANE
IEEE G-MTT International Microwave Symposium
IEEE Intercon75, New York
IEEE MTT-S International Microwave Symposium
If this be error
Ife, William Cox-
IFI Caribbean guidebook
IFIP-ICC vocabulary of information processing
IFIP Symposium on Digital Control . . .
IFIP TC-2 Special Working Conference . . .
IFIP TC 7 optimization conferences
The intelligent heart
INTELSAT: Policy-Maker's dilemma
Intense neutron sources
Ion beams
Ion-molecule reactions
ION/NASA Meeting on Problems in Inertial Guidance
IQSY
Ire, Envye, Accidie or Sloth, Avarice, Glotonye and Lecherye
Ire, Lawrence

6.   NAMES AND PREFIXES

A prefix that is part of the name of a person or place is treated as a separate word unless it is joined to the rest of the name directly or by an apostrophe without a space.

EXAMPLES:
Darby, William
D'Arcy, Ella
Dard, Alfred
De Alberti, Amelia
De Forest, Charlotte
De, Harinath

De Kalb (Ill., U.S.)
De L., E. F.
De la Motte, Carl
De la Ramée
De la Roche
De La Salle, R
De La Torre-Bueno, José
De la Torre, Teofile
De La Tour d' Auvergne, Edouard
De la Tour, Henrie
De Las Casas, Cristobal
De Latour, François
De laudibus Dei
De Morgan, William
De Scribe à Ibsen
De senectute
De'Ath, Wilfred
Death, William
DeCasseres, Benjamin
Defoe, Daniel
Deformation of solids
Del arte de la imprenta en España
Del, Helene
Del idioma universal
Del Mar, Eugene
Dela Mota, F. E.
Delamotte, Freeman
Delasalle, Paul
Delatorre, Haya
Delatour, Jacques
Dell' Acqua Vieytes, Macedonio
Dell' arte dei giardini inglesi
Dell service book
Dell, William
Della-Piana, Gabriel
Della Torre, Luigi
Dellagiovanna, Emil
Dell'arte della parola . . .
Delmar, Dora

Mac   ["see also" reference]
Macalister, Alexander
MacAlister, James
Macaulay, James
Macbeth Gallery, New York
MacCauley, Clay

Macdonald
Mach
Machen
Macheron
Machiavelli
Machinery
MacHugh, Augustin
Macieira, Antonio
Mack, Alexander
MacLaren, Hale
Maclaren, Ian
MacLaren, J
M'Bala
Mc   ["see also" reference]
McAlister, Edward
McAll, Reginald
McAllister, James
McAuley, Mary
McBurney, Ralph
McCalister, Wayde
McCall, Arthur
McCallister, James
McCall's magazine
McHugh, James
McLaren, Jack
M'Ilvaine, William

Van De Graaf, Jan
Van de Mark, Mildred
Van de Velde, Paul
Van Den Berg, Alan
Van den Berg, Lawrence
Van den Bergh, Kas
Van Denburgh, John
Van der Horst, Ulrich
Van der Marck, Jan
Van Derveer, Lettie
Van Dyke, Henry
Van land tot land
Van-Linh
Van Stan, Ina
VanDeMark, Robert
Vanden Berg, Glen
Vandenberg, Arthur
Vander Linde, Arthur
Vandermark, Elzo
Vanderwalker, Fred

7.   NONROMAN ALPHABETS

If, in the arrangement of bibliographic records, it is necessary to distinguish access points containing characters in different nonroman alphabets, scripts, and syllabaries (cf. Rule 1, Order of Characters), the following order of precedence is used:

Amharic	Inuktitut
Arabic	Japanese
Armenian	Kannada
Bengali	Khmer
Burmese	Korean
Chinese	Lao
Coptic	Malayalam
Cree	Manchurian
Cyrillic	Mongolian
Devanagari	Oriya
Georgian	Sinhalese
Glagolitic (Church Slavic)	Syriac
Greek	Tamil
Gujarati	Telugu
Gurmukhi	Thai
Hebrew	Tibetan

8.   NUMERALS
8.1   General Rule

When numeric character strings are compared in order to arrange bibliographic records, they file according to numerical significance from lowest to highest, except as specified in the remainder of Rule 8. Each numeric character string is considered as a whole. It should be remembered, however, that spaces, dashes, hyphens, diagonal slashes, and periods are equivalent and mark the beginning and end of character strings.

8.2   Punctuation

Punctuation used to increase the readability of a numeral (e.g., 2,437,895) is treated as if it did not exist. Punctuation used in other ways (e.g., 1948/49; 1:0; 4-19-69; 3:56) is treated as a space. In the first, fourth, and seventh examples of the following group, the period is used to increase readability. In the first example, the comma is the equivalent of a decimal point.

EXAMPLES:
5.000,25 meter
5,000- and 10,000-year star catalogs
The 5000 and the power tangle
5.000 años de historia
The 5,000 fingers of Dr. T

5000 Jahre Bier
5.000 kilomètres dans le sud
$5,000 reward; or, The missing bride

8.3 Decimals

Numerals after a decimal point are arranged digit by digit, one place at a time. Decimal numerals that are not combined with a whole numeral (e.g., .45) are arranged before the numeral *1*.

EXAMPLES:
.300 Vickers machine gun mechanism
.303-inch machine guns and small arms
'.45-70' rifles
1:0 für Dich
1, 2, buckle my shoe
3.1416 and all that
The 3.2 beer law . . .
3,8 kilometer nach Berlin
3 point 2 and what goes with it
3 vo 365

8.4 Fractions

Characters in fractions are arranged in the following order: numerator, line (the line, whether horizontal or diagonal, is the equivalent of a space), denominator. For filing purposes, fractions combined with whole numerals are considered to be preceded by a space, whether or not one is present.

EXAMPLES:
2½ minute talk treasury
¾ for 3
3/10 for the ladies
3 and 30 watchbirds
21-8-1968: anno humanitatis

8.5 Nonarabic Notation

Numerals in nonarabic notation are interfiled with their arabic equivalents (e.g., XIV is filed as if it were 14).

EXAMPLES:
Louis IX en Égypte
Louis XII, père du peuple
Louis XIV et le Masque de fer
Louis 14th furniture
Louis XV et sa cour
Louis XVI et la révolution

31

Louis XVI und Empire
The Louis Bromfield trilogy
Louis Quatorze
Louis Sinclair
Louis the fifteenth and his times

8.6   Superscript and Subscript Numerals

Superscript and subscript numerals are filed as "on-the-line" numerals. For filing purposes, all superscript and subscript numerals are considered to be preceded by a space.

EXAMPLES (illustrating rules 8 through 8.6):
1:0 für Dich
1:00 a.m.
1,2- dithiolenes
1¾ yards of silk
1.3 acres
1,3- cyclohexadienes
1^3 is 1
⅓ of an inch of French bread
1- bicyclobutylcopper (I) compounds
1 o'clock jump
I. Transfer RNA conformation . . .
2½ % PDQ interest tables
2′, 3′ isomeric specificity
2.5 percent
II-VI semiconducting compounds
2.8% interest
2 + and 3 − states in the even tin isotopes
2 kinetic sculptors
2 phase flows in turbines
2 x 2 = 5
2N calculation
3½ monate Fabrik-arbeitern
3.2 beer for all
3/3's
¾ for 3
3-5-7 minute talks on Freemasonry
3:10 to Yuma
3 a's: art, applied art, architecture
3-D scale drawing
3 point 2 and what goes with it
3 x 3: Stairway to the sea
3M Company
$6.41 per hen per year
6 folk dances from Europe
6- Hydroxydopamine . . .
007. James Bond; a report

10 stars from the 40's
13 is a lucky number
14 MeV Neutron
17 days to better living
XVIIe & XVIIIe siècles
XVIIme siècle
The 17th century
Der 18. Oktober
18 years from now
18th century church architecture
$20 a week
XX century cyclopaedia and atlas
20 humorous stories
XXth century citizen's atlas of the world
25 stories
37 short plays
37$_s$ contamination
49 best short stories
'49 to '94
^{49}Ca contamination
49th parallel
60 American painters, 1960
63 days
90° in the shade
$100 a year
100 years — for what?
150 kleine Garten
150 loyal songs
150th anniversary
200 years of architectural drawing
200T analog computer operation manual
291   [periodical]
600.0245
600 new churches
1000 Chestnut St.
1789
2000 A.D., a documentary
6800 programming for logic design
Double 0 seven. James Bond
N-oxides
Na$_8$
Na$_{12}$ and icosahedral
Na means I in Korean
NH$_4$ I-KI solid solution
Ninety degrees in the shade
One hundred advertising talks
Six chansons gestes
Six, Jan, 1857–1926

Six living poets
Six, Ray L.
Six twenty six; pub. by U.S. Forest Service
Six van Vromade, Jan Willem
Sixty American poets, 1896–1944
Sixty pounds a second on defense
Sixty-Three, pseud.
Three men on a horse
Twentieth Century Limited
Twenty dollars a week
Two and a half centuries of Judaism
Two-stroke power units

8.7 Dates in a Chronological File

Dates in fields such as titles are filed according to Rule 8.1, i.e., by numerical significance.

8.7.1 Dates Expressed in Numerals

In a chronological file (e.g., period subdivisions under the name of a place as subject; personal name with date) dates are arranged according to chronology so that B.C. dates precede A.D. dates in inverse numerical order. Abbreviations such as *b., d.,* and *fl.* in such files are disregarded.

EXAMPLES:
Brown, John, 1610?–1679
Brown, John, 1610–1680
Brown, John, 1696?–1742
Brown, John, 1715–1766
Brown, John, 1800–1859
Brown, John, b. 1817
Brown, John, 1819–1840
Brown, John, d. 1826
Brown, John, 1826–1883
Brown, John, d. 1829
Brown, John, 1847–1930
Brown, John, fl. 1854
Brown, John, 1878–
Brown, John, 1900 March 2–
Brown, John, 1900 July 18–
Brown, John, 1914–
Brown, John A

8.7.2 Incompletely Expressed Dates

A historic time period that is generalized or expressed only in

34

words is treated as if it consisted of the full range of dates for the period. For example, "16th century" is arranged as 1500–1599. Period subdivisions in the form of "To [date]" are arranged before all other dates in the chronological sequence, including B.C. dates. Period subdivisions are arranged chronologically even when the dates do not appear as the first element of that subdivision; "UNITED STATES–HISTORY–CIVIL WAR, 1861–1865" is arranged as "UNITED STATES HISTORY 1861–1865." Geologic time periods are arranged alphabetically.

EXAMPLES:

EGYPT–HISTORY
    –TO 332 B.C.   [0–332 B.C.]
    –TO 640 A.D.   [0–640 A.D.]
    –332–30 B.C.
    –GRAECO-ROMAN PERIOD, 332 B.C.–640 A.D.
    –30 B.C.–640 A.D.
    –640–1250
    –640–1882

UNITED STATES–HISTORY
    –COLONIAL PERIOD, CA. 1600–1775
    –KING WILLIAM'S WAR, 1689–1697
    –QUEEN ANNE'S WAR, 1702–1713
    –FRENCH AND INDIAN WAR, 1755–1763
    –REVOLUTION, 1775–1783
    –CONFEDERATION, 1783–1789
    –1783–1815
    –1783–1865
    –CONSTITUTIONAL PERIOD, 1789–1809
    –1801–1809
    –WAR OF 1812
    –WAR WITH ALGERIA, 1815
    –1815–1861
    –CIVIL WAR, 1861–1865
    –1865–
    –1865–1898
    –1865–1921
    –WAR OF 1898
    –1898–
    –20TH CENTURY   [1900–1999]
    –1901–1953
    –1945–

9.   RELATORS (DESIGNATORS OF FUNCTION) USED IN
      NAME HEADINGS
      Words that show the role of a person or corporate body in rela-
tion to a particular work are disregarded in arranging access points.

EXAMPLES:
Standard Oil Company
   Denials of justice

   Standard Oil Company
Palmer, John
   Digest of laws . . .

   Standard Oil Company, defendant
Ohio, plaintiff
   In the Supreme Court of Ohio

   Standard Oil Company, appellant
Johnson, John
   Standard Oil Company of New Jersey . . . 1960

   Standard Oil Company, appellant
United States, appellee
   Standard Oil Company of New Jersey . . . 1965

   Standard Oil Company, respondent
United States.   Department of Justice
   The United States, petitioner

Standard Oil Company
   Whose oil is it?

   STANDARD OIL COMPANY
Boher, John Calhoun
   Directors and their function

Standard Oil Company.   Committee on Reservoir
      Development and Operation.
   Joint progress report

9.1.   Relators in Name Headings (Optional)
      Words that show the role of a person or a corporate body in a
legal action are regarded in arranging access points. All other relators (designators of function) are disregarded.

EXAMPLES:
Standard Oil Company
   Denials of justice

   Standard Oil Company
Palmer, John
   Digest of laws . . .

Standard Oil Company
  Whose oil is it?

STANDARD OIL COMPANY
Boher, John Calhoun
  Directors and their function

Standard Oil Company, appellant
Johnson, John
  Standard Oil Company of New Jersey . . . 1960

Standard Oil Company, appellant
United States, appellee
  Standard Oil Company of New Jersey . . . 1965

Standard Oil Company.   Committee on Reservoir
    Development and Operation.
  Joint progress report

Standard Oil Company, defendant
Ohio, plaintiff
  In the Supreme Court of Ohio

Standard Oil Company, respondent
United States.   Department of Justice
  The United States, petitioner

10.   TERMS OF HONOR AND ADDRESS

In access points beginning with a surname, all terms of honor and address (e.g., *Dame, Lady, Lord, Sir, Mrs.*) are disregarded for filing purposes. In access points other than those beginning with a surname, terms of honor and address are regarded for filing purposes in the order in which they are present in the heading.

EXAMPLES:
  John II, King of Aragon
  John II, Pope
  John III, Duke of Brabant
  John XXI, Pope
  John, Abbot of Ford
  John, Alois
  John Ambrose, Father
  John, Bishop of Norwich
  John Capistran, Saint
  John Crerar Library, Chicago
  John, Duke of Lancaster
  John, Sir Edward
  John, Elector of Saxony
  John-Ferrer, F
  John Gabriel, Sister

John Gardener, 15th cent.
John, Dr. George
John, Herr
John, King of England
John, Mrs.   [John as a forename]
John o' London
John of Gaddesden
John, of Hildesheim
John-Quill
John, Saint, Apostle
John the Teuton
John, Mrs. William

Appendix I
Modified Letters and Special Characters

As stated in Rule 1.1, modified letters are treated like their plain equivalents in the English alphabet. The following list indicates the filing equivalents for any modified letters or special characters that exist as separate alphabetic characters in the ALA extended character set (also known as the MARC character set).[1] The list does not include any symbols or diacritics that are always used in conjunction with an alphabetic character; such marks are ignored for filing purposes.

Character Name	Symbol	Filing Equivalent
Ligature ae	æ	ae
Slash d	đ	d
Eth	ð	d
Dotless i	ı	i
Slash l	ł	l
Hook o	ơ	o
Slash o	ø	o
Ligature oe	œ	oe
Thorn	þ	th
Hook u	ư	u

1. Published as Appendix III-B in: United States. Library of Congress. Automated Systems Office. *MARC formats for bibliographic data.* — Washington, D.C. : Library of Congress, 1980.

Articles in the Nominative Case in Various Foreign Languages

The following table lists definite and indefinite articles in frequently encountered languages in the nominative case only (all genders, both singular and plural) which should be disregarded according to the rule for initial articles (Rule 4). Under each language they are listed in the following order: singular — masculine, feminine, neuter; plural — same. An elided form follows its corresponding word or group of words; each article is listed only once under each language. The words in parentheses are variants or dialect forms. An alphabetical index to all articles in the table follows the table.

An asterisk (*) before an indefinite article indicates that the same form is also used for the cardinal numeral one; therefore, care must be taken to distinguish the meaning (see Rule 4.2).

Language	*Definite Article*	*Indefinite Article*
Afrikaans	Die	'n
Albanian	See footnote 1	*Një (Nji)
Arabic	al-, el-[2]	None
Bulgarian	See footnote 1	None
Catalan	El, L', La, Els, Les	*Un, *Una
Czech (Bohemian)	No articles	
Danish	Den, Det, De	*En, *Et

1. Albanian, Bulgarian, and Romanian have definite articles, but they are added as suffixes to the word they make definite.

2. The Arabic articles *al* or *el* (or the assimilated forms *ad-, ag-, ak-, an-, ar-, as-, at-, az-)* as initial words of a title, though joined by a hyphen to the word following, are to be disregarded in filing.

Language	Definite Article	Indefinite Article
Dutch	De, Het, 't	*Een, Eene, 'n
English	The	A, An
Esperanto	La	None
Estonian	No articles	
Finnish	No articles	
French	Le, La, L', Les	*Un, *Une
German	Der, Die, Das	*Ein, *Eine
Greek, Classical	Ho, Hē, To, Tō, Hoi, Hai, Ta	None
Greek, Modern	Ho, Hē, To, Hoi, Hai, Ta	*Henas (Heis), *Mia, *Hena (Hen)
Hawaiian	Ka, Ke, Na, O[3]	He
Hebrew	ha-, he-	None
Hungarian	A, Az	*Egy
Icelandic (Modern)	Hinn, Hin, Hio, Hinir, Hinar	None
Italian	Il, Lo, L', La, Gli, Gl', I, Le	Un, *Uno, *Una, Un'
Latin	No articles	
Latvian	No articles	
Lithuanian	No articles	
Norwegian (Bokmål)	Den, Det, De	*En, *Et
Norwegian (Nynorsk)	Den, Det, Dei	*Ein, *Ei, *Eit
Polish	No articles	
Portuguese	O, A, Os, As[4]	*Um, *Uma
Romanian	See footnote 1	*Un, *O
Russian	No articles	
Serbo-Croatian	No articles	
Slovak	No articles	
Slovenian	No articles	
Spanish	El, La, Lo[5], Los, Las	*Un, *Una
Swedish	Den, Det, De	*En, *Ett
Turkish (New)	None	*Bir
Ukrainian	No articles	
Welsh	Y, Yr	None
Yiddish	Der, Di, Die, Dos	A, An, *Ein, *Eine

3. In Hawaiian, the "O emphatic" must be carefully distinguished from the preposition *O*, but *O* also serves the Hawaiian language as a noun and a verb (each with several meanings), an adverb, and a conjunction.

4. In Portuguese the words *à* and *às* with accents are not articles and must be regarded in filing.

5. In Spanish the use of the word *lo* as an article is very restricted and therefore must be carefully distinguished from its other uses.

ALPHABETICAL INDEX TO ARTICLES IN ABOVE TABLE

A	English, Hungarian, Portuguese, Yiddish	Het	Dutch
al	Arabic	Hio	Icelandic
An	English, Yiddish	Hin	
As	Portuguese	Hinar	Icelandic
Az	Hungarian	Hinir	
Bir	Turkish	Hinn	
Das	German	Ho	Greek
De	Danish, Dutch, Norwegian (Bokmàl), Swedish	Hoi	Greek
		I	Italian
Dei	Norwegian (Nynorsk)	Il	Italian
Den	Danish, Norwegian, Swedish	Ka	Hawaiian
Der	German, Yiddish	Ke	Hawaiian
Det	Danish, Norwegian, Swedish	L'	Catalan, French, Italian
Di	Yiddish	La	Catalan, Esperanto, French, Italian, Spanish
Die	Afrikaans, German, Yiddish	Las	Spanish
Dos	Yiddish	Le	French, Italian
Een	Dutch	Les	Catalan, French
Eene		Lo	Italian, Spanish
Egy	Hungarian	Los	Spanish
Ei	Norwegian (Nynorsk)	Mia	Greek, Modern
Ein	German, Norwegian (Nynorsk), Yiddish	'n	Afrikaans, Dutch
		Na	Hawaiian
Eine	German, Yiddish	Një	Albanian
Eit	Norwegian (Nynorsk)	Nji	
el-	Arabic	O	Hawaiian, Portuguese, Romanian
El	Catalan, Spanish		
Els	Catalan	Os	Portuguese
En	Danish, Norwegian (Bokmål), Swedish	't	Dutch
		Ta	Greek
Et	Danish, Norwegian (Bokmal)	The	English
		To	Greek
Ett	Swedish	Tō	Greek, Classical
Gl'	Italian	Um	Portuguese
Gli		Uma	
ha-	Hebrew	Un	Catalan, French, Italian, Romanian, Spanish
Hai	Greek	Un'	
He	Hawaiian	Una	Catalan, Italian, Spanish
Hē	Greek	Une	French
he-	Hebrew	Uno	Italian
Heis	Greek, Modern	Y, Yr	Welsh
Hen	Greek, Modern		
Hena			
Henas			

42

Glossary

Abbreviation. A shortened form of a written word or phrase, which is used for brevity in place of the whole; commonly made by omission of letters from one or more parts of the whole.

Access Point. A data element placed at the head of a catalog entry to provide access to that entry in a catalog.

Acronym. A word formed from the initial letter or letters of each of the successive parts or major parts of a compound name.

Author-title added entry. *See* Name-title added entry.

Bibliographic record. One or more data elements describing and identifying an item or group of items held by a library, e.g., an entry in a catalog.

Character. A graphic symbol used as a unit in writing or printing.

Collective uniform title. A conventional title used to collocate publications of an author, composer, or corporate body containing several works or extracts from several works, e.g., Piano music (MARC fields 240 and 243, all subfields). For filing purposes this title, if present, is used instead of a romanized title or the title proper for subarranging records.

Data element. One or more words, phrases, or character strings representing a distinct unit of bibliographic information and forming part of a bibliographic record.

Entry. (1) An access point. (2) A bibliographic record found under a particular access point in a catalog.

Field. Units of information within a bibliographic record, e.g., author, title, imprint, added entry, as used in the MARC formats.

Filing title. *See* Uniform title 2.

Filing value. The relative significance assigned to spaces, numerals, letters, and other printed or written signs and symbols for purposes of arrangement of bibliographic records. *See* Rule 1 in text.

Heading. *See* Access point.

Initialism. A group of characters, which may or may not be separated by punctuation marks and/or spaces, formed from the initial letter or letters of each of the successive parts or major parts of a compound name. An initialism, unlike an acronym, is not pronounced as a word.

Main entry. The principal access point for a bibliographic record. *See also* Title main entry.

Name-title added entry. An added entry consisting of the name of a person or corporate body and the title of an item. For filing purposes the name portion consists of all words up to the title (MARC subfields occurring before $t); the title portion consists of all the remaining words (MARC subfields $t and following).

Numerical significance. The quantitative value of a character string consisting in whole or in part of numbers.

Record. *See* Bibliographic record.

Romanized title. A title formed by transliteration into the roman alphabet of a title in a nonroman alphabet (MARC field 241, all subfields). For filing purposes this title, if present, is used instead of the title proper for subarranging records.

Sign. A conventional mark or device having a recognized particular meaning and used in place of words; an ideographic mark, figure, or picture conventionally used in writing or printing to represent a technical term or conception.

Symbol. An arbitrary or conventional sign used in writing or printing relating to a particular field (such as mathematics, physics, chemistry, music, or phonetics) to represent operations, quantities, spatial position, valence, direction, elements, relations, qualities, sounds, or other ideas or qualities.

Title. Any word, phrase, or group of characters naming an item. For filing purposes it includes: uniform title (MARC fields 240 and 243, all subfields); romanized title (MARC field 241, all subfields); and title proper, including short title, name and designation of part or sections, inclusive and bulk dates (for manuscripts) (MARC field 245, subfields a, n, p, f, and g). *See also* Title added entry, Title main entry.

Title added entry. An added entry consisting of a title. For filing purposes it includes MARC field 210 (all subfields); 212 (all subfields); 222 (all subfields); 241 (all subfields); 242 (subfields a, n, and p); 245 (subfields a, n, p, f, and g); 246 and 247 (subfields a, n, and p); 440 (subfields a, n, p, and v); 740 (all subfields); and 840 (all subfields).

Title heading. *See* Title added entry, Title main entry.

Title main entry. A main entry with no author or uniform title serving as author.

For filing purposes it includes MARC fields 240 (all subfields), 241 (all subfields), and 245 (subfields a, n, p, f, and g), providing there is no 1XX present.

Title proper. The chief name of an item. For filing purposes it includes the short title, name, and designation of part or sections, inclusive and bulk dates (for manuscripts) (MARC field 245, subfields a, n, p, f, and g).

Uniform title. (1) The particular title specified for a work with no known author that has appeared under various titles. This uniform title takes the place of an author (MARC field 130, all subfields). (2) The particular title specified for a work with an author that has appeared under various titles (MARC field 240, all subfields). For filing purposes this title, if present, is used instead of a romanized title or the title proper for subarranging records. *See also* Collective uniform title, Uniform title added entry.

Uniform title added entry. An added entry consisting of a uniform title. For filing purposes it includes MARC fields 243 (all subfields), 630 (all subfields), 730 (all subfields except $x), and 830 (all subfields).

Word. (1) A speech sound or series of speech sounds that symbolizes and communicates a meaning without being divisible into smaller units capable of independent use. (2) In particular for these rules, a written or printed character or combination of characters representing a spoken word; especially, any segment of written or printed discourse ordinarily appearing between spaces or between a space and a punctuation mark. Used synonomously with *character string.*

Index

References are to rule numbers unless otherwise designated.

A
as initial article, 4.1, 4.2
as the cardinal numeral one, p. 24, p. 40–41
A.D. dates, 8.7.1
Abbreviations, 3; p. 5
definition, Glossary
see also Acronyms, Initials
Accent marks, 1.1
Access points, 2
definition, Glossary
function of, 2.2
identical, 2.4
in nonroman alphabets, 7
not identical, 2.1
subarrangement, 2.3, 2.3.1; tables 1 & 2
terms of honor and address, 10
see also Added entries, Author entries, Series entries, Subject entries, Title entries
Acronyms, 5; p. 5
definition, Glossary
Added entries, 2, 2.2, 2.3; table 1
optional arrangement, 2.3.1; table 2
references for, 2.2
see also Name-title added entry
Additions to personal names, 2.1.1, 10
Address, terms of, 2.1.1, 10
Alphabet, English, 1, 1.1
Alphabets, nonroman, 1
priority order, 7
Ampersand, 1.2, 1.3
see also Special characters
An, as initial article, 4.1, 4.2

Apostrophes, in names with a prefix, 6
Arrangement guides, p. 5, 8; fig. 5
Articles, initial, 2.1.1, 4, 4.1, 4.2
at beginning of nickname or sobriquet, 4.1
elided, 4.2
list of foreign articles, p. 40–42
part of personal and place names, 4.1
part of subject subdivisions, p. 24, note 5; fig. 3
part of titles, 4.2
part of topical subjects, 4.2
see also A
Asterisks, examples under 1.2
Author entries, arrangement, 2.3; fig. 5; table 1
Author-title entry,
see Name-title added entry

b., as abbreviation, 8.7.1
B.C. dates, 8.7.1, 8.7.2
Bible, p. 8
Bibliographical records
arrangement by nonroman alphabets, scripts, or syllabaries, 7
definition, Glossary
function, 2.2

Categorical references, p. 5; fig. 1
Character strings, 1, 5; p. 2, p. 3
numeric, 8.1
Characters
definition, Glossary
form, 2.1.1

Characters *(Con't.)*
  in decimal numbers, 8.3
  in fractions, 8.4
  order, 1, 2.1, 2.1.1
  see also Special characters
Chronological files, 8.7, 8.7.1, 8.7.2
Collective uniform titles, 2.3.1; fig. 5
  definition, Glossary
Corporate names, 2.1.2, 2.3; table 1
  initial articles, 4.1

d., as abbreviation, 8.7.1
Dame (in name headings), 10
Dashes, 1; examples under 1.2, 5, 8.1; p. 2,
  p. 9
Data elements, 2.1.2
  definition, Glossary
  identical, 2.4
  subarrangement, 2.3; p. 16–18; table 1
Date of publication, distribution, etc., 2.3,
  2.3.1; tables 1 & 2
Dates
  expressed as numerals, 8.7.1
  expressed in words, 8.7.2
  in chronological files, 8.7
  in personal name headings, 8.7.1
  incompletely expressed, 8.7.2
  see also Geologic time periods, Numerals
Decimals, 8.2, 8.3
Diacritical marks, 1.1; p. 39
Diagonal slashes, 1, 5, 8.1; p. 2, p. 9
Dollar signs, 1.2

El, example under 4.2
Elided prefixes, names with, examples
  under 6
Elisions, 4.2
English alphabet, 1, 1.1
Entries
  definition, Glossary
  see Access points
Etc., as abbreviation, examples under 3

Field, definition, Glossary
"File-as-is" principle, p. 1, p. 2
Filing order, 2.2, 2.3; p. 2
Filing title, *see* Uniform title
Filing value, definition, Glossary
fl., as abbreviation, 8.7.1
Fractions, 8.4
Full stops, *see* Periods
Function designators, 9, 9.1

Geologic time periods, 8.7.2
Geographic names, *see* Place names

Headings
  definition, Glossary
  see Access points
Honor and address, terms of, 2.1.1, 10
Hyphenated words, p. 5
Hyphens, 1; p. 2, p. 9; examples under 1.2,
  5, 8.1

"ignored," definition, p. 9, note 1
Imprint date, *see* Date of publication,
  distribution, etc.
Information notices, p. 4–5
  see also References
Initial articles, 2.1.1, 4, 4.1, 4.2
  at beginning of nickname or sobriquet,
    4.1
  elided, 4.2
  list of foreign articles, p. 40–41
  part of personal and place names, 4.1
  part of subject subdivisions, p. 8, note 5;
    fig. 3
  part of titles, 4.2
  part of topical subjects, 4.2
  see also A
Initialisms, 5
  definition, Glossary
Initials, 5; p. 5

K., as abbreviation, examples under 3

Lady (in name headings), 10
Language designations, p. 8; fig. 5
Las, example under 4.2
Lord (in name headings), 10

M., as abbreviation, example under 3
M', as prefix, example under 6
Mac, example under 6
Main entries, 2.2, 2.3, 2.3.1; table 1
  definition, Glossary
  references for, 2.2
MARC fields, 2, 2.3, 4.1, 4.2; p. 16, note 3;
  tables 1 & 2
Mc, example under 6
Mlle., as abbreviation, example under 3
Mme., as abbreviation, example under 3
Modified letters, 1.1; p. 39
Mr., as abbreviation, example under 3
Mrs., as abbreviation, example under 3

Ms., as abbreviation, example under 3

Name entries, 2.3, 2.3.1
  designators of function, 9, 9.1
  see also Corporate names, Personal
    names
Name-title added entry, 2.1.2, 2.3
  definition, Glossary
Nicknames, 4.1
No., as abbreviation, example under 3
Nonroman alphabets, 1
  priority order, 7
Numbers, *see* Numerals
Numerals, 1, 8
  arrangement, 8.1
  decimals, 8.3
  expressed as digits, p. 2, p. 5; fig. 1
  expressed as words, p. 2, p. 5; fig. 1
  fractions, 8.4
  in names of military units, fig. 2
  in nonarabic notation, 8.5
  one same as indefinite article, 4.2
  punctuation, 8.2
  roman, 8.5; fig. 1
  subscript, 8.6
  superscript, 8.6
  see also Dates
Numerical significance, definition,
  Glossary

Order of characters, 1, 2.1, 2.1.1

Parts of a work, p. 8
Performers, 2.3.1
Periods, 1, 5, 8.1; p. 2, p. 9
Personal names, 2.3; p. 3; table 1
  additions to, 2.1.1, 10
  dates in, 8.7.1
  with prefix, 6
Place names, p. 3
  period subdivisions in place names used
    as subjects, 8.7.1
  with prefix, 6
Prefixes, 6; p. 5
Publication data, p. 8
  see also Date of publication,
    distribution, etc.
Punctuation, 1.2; p. 3
  in numerals, 8.2

R., as abbreviation, examples under 3

References, 2.2; p. 4
  categorical references, p. 5; fig. 1
  "see also" references, 2.2
  "see" references, 2.2; fig. 3
  specific filing references, p. 5; figs. 2,
    3 & 4
  see also Arrangement guides
Relators used in name headings, 2.1.1, 9,
  9.1
Romanized titles, 2.3; p. 16, note 3; table 1
  definition, Glossary
  initial articles, 4.2

"See also" references, 2.2
  see also References
"See" references, 2.2; fig. 3
  see also References
Series entries, 2, 2.2, 2.3; p. 3; table 1
  initial articles, 4.2
  references for, 2.2
Signs, 1.2
  definition, Glossary
Sir (in name headings), 10
Slashes, 1, 5, 8.1; p. 2, p. 9
Sobriquets, 4.1
Spaces, 1, 5, 8.1; p. 2, p. 9
Special characters, 1.2; p. 39
St., as abbreviation, example under 3
Ste., as abbreviation, example under 3
Subject entries, 2, 2.2, 2.3; p. 3; table 1
  topical, initial articles, 4.2
Subject subdivisions, p. 3
  initial articles in, example under 4.2;
    fig. 3
  period subdivisions under place names,
    8.7.1, 8.7.2
Symbols, 1.2
  definition, Glossary

Terms of honor and address, 2.1.1, 10
The, as initial article, 4.1, 4.2
Title, definition, Glossary
Title added entry, definition, Glossary
Title entries, 2, 2.3; p. 3; table 1
  arrangement under author, 2.1.2; fig. 5
  collective uniform titles, 2.3, 2.3.1; fig. 5
  dates in title fields, 8.7
  initial articles, 4.2
  optional arrangement, 2.3.1
  see also Uniform titles
Title main entry, definition, Glossary
Title proper, 2.3; p. 16, note 3
  definition, Glossary

Umlaut, examples under 1.1
Uniform title added entry, definition,
   Glossary
Uniform titles, 2.3; p. 5, p. 8; examples
   under 2.3; table 1
   collective uniform title, 2.3.1; examples
      under 2.3.1; table 2
   definition, Glossary
   initial articles, 4.2

nondistinctive, 2.3.1; table 2
see also Title entries

Voluminous authors, p. 5; fig. 5

Word, 5; p. 2
   definition, Glossary
   see also Character strings

Designed by Vladimir Reichl
Composed by Precision Typographers in
   Times Roman on Compugraphic's Unisetter
   with Handel Gothic display type

Printed in the United States
53871LVS00005B/235-309

9 780838 932551